Contents

Will It Rain on Wednesday?

Written by Dorothy Avery • Illustrated by Bruce Potter

"Will it rain on Wednesday?"
asked Jed.
"We're going to the zoo
on Wednesday."

"Let's look in the paper
and see what it says," said Mum.

Monday

3

Jed and Mum looked
in the paper.
"It says rain on Tuesday,"
said Mum. "It could be sunny
by Wednesday."

4

"It's raining again," said Jed. "Will it be sunny by Wednesday?"

"Let's turn on the TV and see what it says," said Mum.

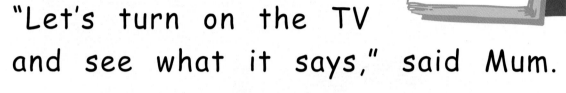

5

Jed and Mum looked
at the TV.
"It says some rain today,
but it could be sunny
on Wednesday," said Mum.

"Mum, Mum, it's sunny today," shouted Jed. "We can go to the zoo!"

Wednesday

7

RAINY DAY

Help the children
use the letters
to make some words.

10

Make a Pizza

1

2

3

4

The Rain

Pitter-patter, raindrops,
falling from the sky.

Here is my umbrella
to keep me safe and dry.

When the rain is over,
and the sun begins to glow,

little flowers start to bud,
and grow
and grow
and grow.

Weather Word Find

Use the pictures
to find seven words.

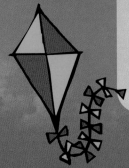

h	d	s	u	n	l	p	b
r	x	a	m	c	d	n	o
a	w	c	b	u	h	e	o
i	p	e	r	m	h	a	t
n	e	c	e	a	w	j	s
c	d	t	l	k	i	t	e
g	q	v	l	e	n	f	o
f	u	y	a	t	d	s	z

12

WORD GAME

Now make your own cards and make some more words.

The Rainy Day BOX

Written by Jean Bennett
Photographed by Mary Foley

I looked out the window
at the rain.

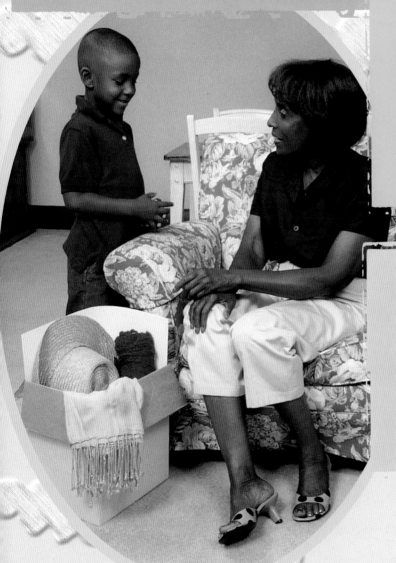

"What can
I do today?"
I asked
Grandma.

"Look in
the Rainy
Day box,"
she said.

I looked in the Rainy Day box.
I found...

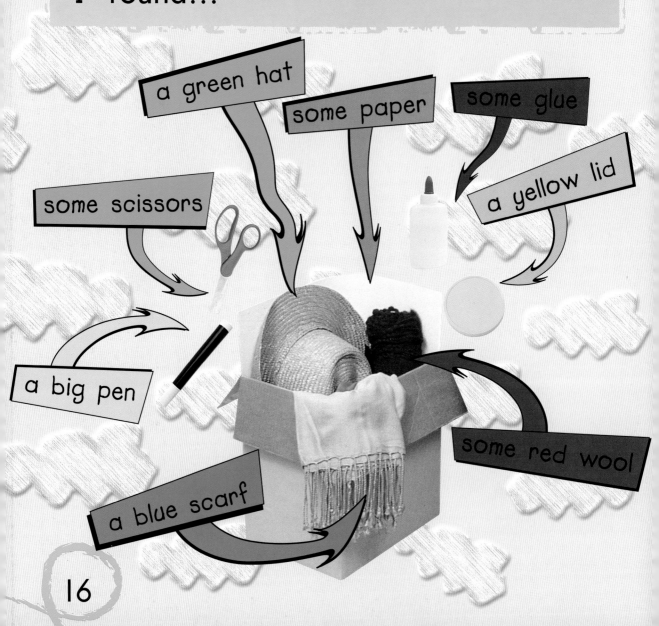

a green hat

some paper

some glue

some scissors

a yellow lid

a big pen

a blue scarf

some red wool

I cut the blue scarf into bits.
I stuck the blue bits
on the paper.

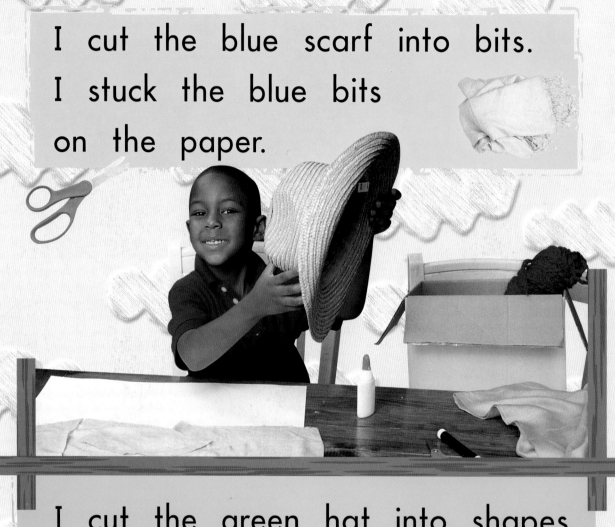

I cut the green hat into shapes.
I stuck the green shapes
on the paper.

I cut the red wool into bits.
I stuck the red bits
on the paper.

I stuck the yellow lid
on the paper.
I drew a big smile
on the yellow lid.

I stuck the paper on the wall.
The yellow sun smiled
in the blue sky.
The yellow sun smiled
on the green hills.
The yellow sun smiled
on the red flowers.

And Grandma and I smiled, too.

An Afternoon of Alphabets

Can you find...
an amazing A,
an emerald E,
an interesting I,
an orange O,
and an unhappy U?

What could you say about...
the letter P,
the letter S,
the letter T,
and the letter Z?

22

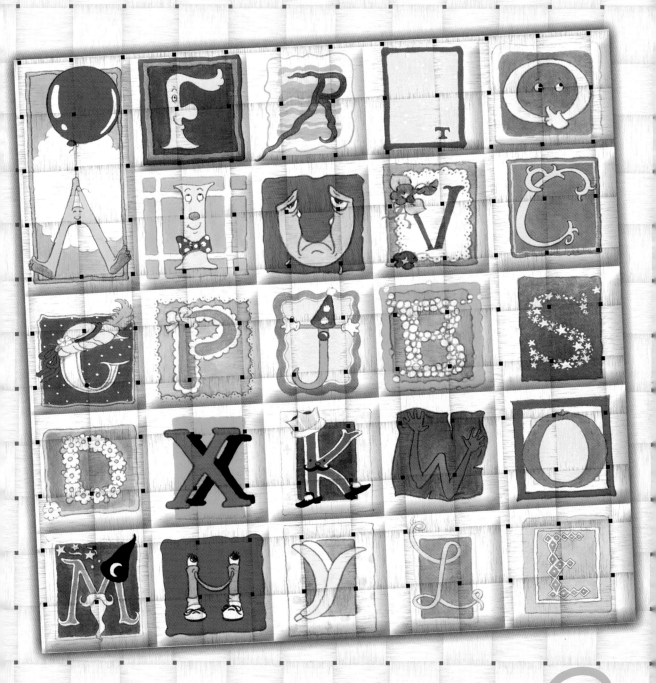

23

The Bit of String

Written by Elizabeth Pulford • Illustrated by Yukari Kakita

Sara looked at the bit of string.

"What can I do with this?" she asked.

"You could play with the kitten like this," said Dad.

26

"You could
tie a tail
on your kite like this," said Mum.

27

"You could play
cat's cradle
like this,"
said Grandpa.

28

Sara looked at the bit of string.

"I could play
with the kitten."

"I could tie
a tail on my kite."

"I could play cat's cradle."

"Or," said Sara,
"I could thread
some beads like this."

31

Then they fall down as rain.

When the sun comes out, the water changes into steam.

Then it starts all over again.

The steam goes up, up, up.
It changes back into drops of water.

The sun is out!

Now we're getting smaller!

Look! We're turning into steam.

Here we go again!

33

Rain, Rain, Stay Away

Rain, rain, stay away.
You can come another day.

Daddy wants
to cut the hay.

May and I
want to play.

So, rain, rain, stay away.
You can come another day.

Letters I Know

 Xx Yy

Sounds I Know

 -ay away, day, play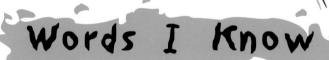

Words I Know

asked	can	of	today
at	could	said	what
be	it	says	will
by	looked	this	with